Reverend Dr. R.B. Holmes, Jr.

The "12 Point Action Plan Vision" for

Revitalizing the National Baptist Convention, USA, Inc.

Ronald W. Holmes, Ph.D.

Publisher, The Holmes Education Post, LLC

"An Education Focused Internet Newspaper"

authorHOUSE®

AuthorHouse™
1663 Liberty Drive
Bloomington, IN 47403
www.authorhouse.com
Phone: 1-800-839-8640

Scripture taken from the King James Version of the Bible.

Published by AuthorHouse 06/19/2014

ISBN: 978-1-4969-1856-7 (sc)
ISBN: 978-1-4969-1854-3 (e)

Table of Contents

ACKNOWLEDGEMENT

Reverend Dr. R.B. Holmes Jr. is an extraordinary pastor and visionary leader for this millennium. Holmes' strong family background, extensive community service activities and church experiences as a pastor for 37 years, past president of the National Baptist Congress of Christian Education for 10 years and past president of Congress of Christian Education for the Florida General Baptist Convention for six years have led him to become president of the National Baptist Convention USA, Inc. (National Baptist Convention). Consequently, I am happy to write this book to support his presidency, as well as to serve as a model to support the needs of churches of the National Baptist Convention.

On Tuesday, January 21, 2014, Reverend Holmes was announced and certified officially to become a candidate of The National Baptist Convention. Holmes was accompanied by his wife Dr. Gloria Holmes and a host of pastors across the country who support his candidacy. Some of these persons included: Reverend Dr. Cullian Hill; Reverend Dr. Thurman B. Everett; Reverend Dr. Leonard T. King; Reverend Dr. Roosevelt T. Joyner and Reverend Dr. Jimmy L. Brown.

On March 25, 2014, Reverend Holmes announced his candidacy for the National Baptist Convention USA, Inc. at the National Press Club in Washington, D.C. Holmes believes that we can create and develop a holistic model to transform The World Baptist Center into a full service ministry operation for supporting local Baptist churches and providing solutions to address the spiritual, social, educational and economic challenges of the 21st Century. Notable community and professional leaders across the nation were in attendance and gave presentations of their roles in support of Holmes' candidacy. Some of these supporters included the Honorable Judge Glenda Hatchett, Attorney Benjamin Crump, Reverend Dr. Jamal Bryant, Reverend Dr. Cullian Hill, the parents of the late Robert Champion, Travon Martin, Jordan Davis and Michael Jiles.

Thus, Reverend Holmes' dedication and commitment to family, church and community is needed in a 21st Century economy to rebuild and reinvigorate the National Baptist Convention. I am sincerely happy to write this book to support Holmes' efforts to become president of the convention. I would like to thank all the pastors, particularly Reverend Dr. John H. Grant, and other constituents for providing their comments to support the book. I would also like to thank my wife, Constance Holmes, for being the editor for the book.

DEDICATION

We dedicate this book to Reverend Dr. R.B. Holmes Jr. in his pursuit of the presidency for the National Baptist Convention USA, Inc. All proceeds will benefit Historically Black Colleges and Universities affiliated with the National Baptist Convention USA, Inc.

It is our hope that this book will help to support Reverend Holmes' candidacy and serve as a model to address the needs of churches particularly associated with the convention.

For centuries, there has been a debate about whether leaders are born or made. Some people believe leaders are born because they have inherited an innate ability to effectively manage an organization. Others believe leaders are made because they have to apply their prior and current experiences to each new leadership position. What is clear is that, effective leaders are resulted-oriented who understands the essential components for running an organization.

Reverend Holmes has consistently proven his effectiveness in leading, facilitating, guiding and managing a plethora of organizations with measurable results. Given the opportunity to apply his wealth of knowledge, skills and understanding to the National Baptist Convention, he will bring prosperity and hope to people throughout the world.

So, let's give him a chance!

TRIBUTE to Reverend Dr. R.B. Holmes Jr.

By Ashaki Noni Holmes-Kidd, daughter

"The heart of a father is the masterpiece of nature."
— Antoine François Prévost, Manon Lescaut

The quote above perfectly sums up what I think about my father, Rev. Dr. R.B. Holmes, Jr. In my eyes, he is truly a masterpiece. He is loving, understanding, protective, and has a sense of humor to boot - the perfect mix for a wonderful father. Despite his hectic schedule, he has always been incredibly supportive of every endeavor I have undertaken throughout my life. It feels really good to know that I will always have him in my corner no matter what.

I realize, however, that having such an awesome father is not the norm. In fact, when searching for the quote above, I was shocked (though, sadly, not surprised) by the number of negative quotes I found about the decline of fatherhood in our society. This search brought to light one of the core issues that we are facing as a country and as a people: the presence of loving and supportive fathers has diminished exponentially and, in some communities, is virtually non-existence.

Recognizing the importance of his father in his life and how important he is to me and my siblings, my dad has worked relentlessly for much of his almost four decade career to help strengthen families. At his church, Bethel Missionary Baptist Church, he has developed numerous innovative mentoring and educational programs and ministries that focus on instilling traditional values in youth that will enable them to become productive, responsible citizens and, ultimately, great parents. One such program is the recently opened all-male academy for elementary and middle school boys.

It should be no surprise then that one of my dad's central platforms for his campaign for the presidency of the National Baptist Convention USA, Inc. is focused on restoring the African-American family. He has already made efforts in this regard through the

National Save The Family Now Movement, Inc., an organization that he founded a few years ago that has received recognition throughout the country from government officials and respected corporations for its timely mission. In other words, my dad has a proven track record of working to re-build families and has done this effectively and efficiently for decades.

By all accounts, one could say that my dad has had a successful career. He has received countless awards, accolades, and recognition throughout his career, but one thing that I most respect and admire about him is his humility. I have never heard him discuss with others his many achievements and successes because those things are not important to him. What is important to him is spreading the Word of God throughout this great country to improve the plight of not just African-Americans but every person dwelling herein. What is important to him is striving each day to be a great family man and an even greater man of God.

Therefore, it is with great confidence that I can assure you that a vote for my father is a vote for a man who does not measure his successes by the certificates on his wall, the number of parishioners who attend his church, nor the amount of money in his bank account. A vote for my father is a vote for a man who has dedicated his life to preaching the Gospel and whose walk with God is undeniable. A vote for my father is a vote for a man who is a true visionary and who will continue to work tirelessly to get our families back intact. But, perhaps most importantly, a vote for my father is a vote for a God-fearing man who has been and continues to be a loving son, a supportive father and grandfather, an adoring husband, a caring brother, a doting uncle, a selfless pastor, and an active and dedicated member of his community.

In sum, a vote for my father is a vote for a man who has a heart that is truly a masterpiece of nature.

I love you, Daddy. And I am so proud to be your daughter.

TRIBUTE to Reverend Dr. R.B. Holmes Jr.

By Barbara H. Powell, sister

I have had the awesome pleasure of watching the Reverend Dr. R.B. Holmes, Jr. mature and become one of the most dynamic men I know. He is a man of excellence, ethics, integrity, purpose and vision. As a child, he wanted to be a preacher. I remember when he made the announcement to our family. R.B. Jr. was only seven. Our grandfather having sensed that R.B. Jr. had a special calling for his life, purchased his first Bible. He could barely read; however, by the time he reached his teenage years, that Bible was tattered from all the reading and studying he had done. He was called to the ministry during his sophomore year of college. His first sermon was extremely powerful and dynamic.

As early as first grade, my brother had asthma. He would have asthma attacks at home and when visiting our grandparents for vacation in Georgia. He was repeatedly rushed to the hospital emergency room. However, R.B. Jr. always stated that with the help of God and his strong faith, he would become healthier. He has always believed in God's amazing grace and healing power. Consequently, he overcame asthma.

In high school, R.B. Jr. always had a part time job and would share his money with his siblings, enabling us to have extra lunch money. He has always been very generous, and a natural born leader. He was a high school quarterback and the pitcher on the baseball team. He also had an acting role in his high school senior play. He was a community organizer in our neighborhood, ensuring that the young people were involved in community issues. He's always available whenever you need him and offers, good sound advice. He is very passionate about his beliefs, making every situation better. He has always been a visionary, forward thinker, with excellent ideas.

R.B. Jr. is the third sibling of eight children. In his early years, he was surrounded by sisters, two older and three younger. I think one of the happiest days of his young life was when his two brothers were born: Glen and Ronald. They both followed him to the park and participated in Little League Baseball along with him. To some degree,

6

they emulated him in other areas. Glen is a teacher, football and baseball coach. Ronald is a speaker, educator and author.

His five sisters (Josephine, Barbara, Bettye, Deborah and Sharon) also look up to him and appreciate his unwavering advice and spiritual guidance. Our sister, the late Josephine, took his suggestions and became a superior court judge. Our parents, the late R.B. Sr. and Lucille Holmes were always overjoyed when he came home to visit them. He lit up a room with his sense of humor and graciousness.

My brother has always put God first in his life. He loves his wife Gloria and is a loving father to his children: Tina, Ashaki, Stacey, Embry (son-in-law) and his grandchildren. He's an outstanding pastor and appreciates and loves his members of Bethel Missionary Baptist Church. Because of his many accomplishments, ministries and untiring commitment to all humankind, we love him and wholeheartedly support his presidency for the National Baptist Convention USA, Inc. "And we know that in all things God works for the good of those who love him who have been called according to his purpose:" Roman 8: 28.

FOREWORD

This book is written to serve as a model to support the needs of the churches of the National Baptist Convention USA, Inc., which has a reported membership of eight million members. Since the Convention exists to serve the churches, and not the other way around, and since without the churches, there would be no Convention, it is, therefore, the needs of the churches that are paramount.

Writing in a locally Black-owned newspaper (www.theurbannews.com), an active member of the congregation I serve made an insightful observation regarding the needs of churches. In lamenting over whatever happened to our local Black community, my member noted:

> The only institution that might make some change in this community is the Black church. She has the influence, the property, and some of the capital to make a difference. In this day and time, however, the church has its own problems to contend with. Church membership is falling significantly. Old members pass away, and unlike days gone by, are not being replaced by the next generation. People do not value church like in the past. Those who do are torn because it seems that church is an oligarchy benefiting a few at the expense of the many. Solve these problems, come together regardless of denomination, and the local black community will rise.

I believe my member refrains from overtly naming what he regards as the benefiting few in his article because of the respect he is known to have for his church and pastor. However, the benefiting few he obviously has in mind are the pastors and/or ministers of churches. The perception of the church as an oligarchy benefiting a few at the expense of the many is prevalent, not only in the larger communities where many churches serve, but also throughout many congregations as well. I hear that perception expressed regularly in my interaction with parishioners of many different churches. This perception, however, is one about which many pastors both inside and outside of our Convention seem to be in denial. Such denial is not helping the needs of our churches.

Ironically, if the needs of churches are to be met, then churches have to meet the needs of the many and be perceived as doing so. In words attributed to Jesus in all three of the Synoptic Gospels, the church saves its life by losing it in service to others (Matthew 16:25, Mark 8:35, Luke 9:24).

Losing itself in service to others means ministering holistically and recognizing that the gospel does not single out "spiritual" needs and speak only to those, neither does it single out "social" or "physical" needs and speaks only to those. Churches should speak to the total needs of persons. There should be no strict line of demarcation between holiness and decent housing; between salvation and starvation; between evangelism, education, and economics; between spiritual justification, social justice and jobs; between our spiritual mission and human misery (Luke 4:18-19, Mark 14:16).

It is unbiblical for churches to overly spiritualize our mission in a way that ignores the physical, psychological, and emotional misery of hurting people all around us. In a word, people do need salvation for their souls, but they also need food for their stomachs. Those who are heavenly minded in the biblical context will not neglect doing all the earthly good they can for all the people they can for as long as they can.

The Reverend Doctor R. B. Holmes, Jr., 2014 candidate for President of the National Baptist Convention, USA, Inc., has outlined in his 12 Point Action Plan campaign platform a vision designed to serve as a roadmap to lead this Convention in holistically meeting the needs of the many, the masses, of our churches and communities. (See www.gobig4holmes2014.org)

One may observe the fruit of his labor in the Lord and his visionary leadership as pastor of the Bethel Church in Tallahassee for 27 years and as President of the National Baptist Congress of Christian Education for 10 years. It will then become clear that what he proposes in his presidential platform reflects what he has already done and is doing. The platform is not based on theory but practice – what has been and is actually happening in his ministry.

The Bethel model is so captivating and exemplary that a major national and international philanthropic foundation, the Casey Foundation, has designated that model as a "Community of Hope" in recognition of Bethel's ministries in strengthening, sustaining, and saving families.

I have served as a Missionary Baptist pastor for forty years, and as a convention and denominational leader for most of those years. I have witnessed Dr. Holmes' impeccable character and integrity. I have observed first-hand the fruits of his visionary and anointed leadership in the Lord. I am, accordingly, convinced that the initiatives of the Holmes vision are pregnant with potential and possibilities for the transformation of the National Baptist Convention, USA, Inc., inclusive of its constituent churches, and the communities served by these churches throughout America and beyond.

The hope is that as you read this book, you will be informed and inspired, and that it will be a means which motivates you onward to greater and unprecedented levels of excellence in addressing the unmet needs of the masses in our churches and communities.

Reverend Dr. John H. Grant
Mt. Zion Missionary Baptist Church of Asheville, Inc.
Asheville, North Carolina

INTRODUCTION

The National Baptist Convention USA, Inc. is the largest predominantly African-American Christian denomination in the United States with its headquarters located at the Baptist World Center in Nashville, Tennessee. The National Baptist Convention is reported as having millions of members representing churches, district associations and state conventions throughout the U.S. and abroad. During its historic legacy (1880 – 2014), the convention has had 17 presidents beginning with Rev. W. H. McAlpine from 1880 - 1882 to Rev. Julius R. Scruggs from 2010 – 2014. While there have been numerous challenges plaguing the convention such as organizational, fiscal and managerial, the convention has continued to serve God's people through preaching and teaching.

A person who wishes to become a member or serve as president of the National Baptist Convention must be a constituent member of the convention and in good standing with the constituent membership such as a church, district association or state convention. For the election of president of the National Baptist Convention, "each church, district association or state convention (entity) may be eligible to cast up to five votes," according to the National Baptist Convention. On September 1 – 5, 2014, the election for president of the convention will be held during the 134th annual session in New Orleans, Louisiana.

"Each entity is granted one vote for each year it has registered with the parent body of the convention with at least the minimum registration fee for a church, district association or state convention in each of the following years: 2010, 2011, 2012, 2013 and 2014. The entity must have accumulated a minimum of two votes to participate in the election. Specifically, the entity must have registered, at minimum, in 2014 and at least one other year between 2010 and 2013. The entity must be registered for the 2014 annual session with at least the minimum registration to cast their vote(s) in the election," according to National Baptist Convention.

On Tuesday, January 21, 2014, Reverend Dr. R.B. Holmes Jr. was officially approved by the National Baptist Convention as a candidate for president of the convention. Holmes said that after much prayer and reflection, he decided to seek the presidency of the National Baptist Convention, USA, Inc. Holmes strongly and humbly believes that he has the vision, strength, gifts and experience to build and re-energize the legacy of the National Convention. Holmes believes he has the right spirit, attitude and leadership skills to lead the National Convention to prosperity. Holmes notes that we are living in some critical and challenging times, and it is important that the National Baptist Convention becomes a stronger voice and have a compelling vision that will save, strengthen and sustain Black Baptist churches. Holmes believes that he can lead this National Convention to provide ministries and services that will meet the needs of our churches in the 21st century.

As it is written, "Where there is no vision, the people perish" (Proverbs 29:18). "Our beloved members and churches are hurting" according to Holmes; therefore, he believes that we need a stronger and more vibrant National Convention presence and programs. Holmes firmly believes that the Lord, Jesus Christ, has uniquely prepared him to serve "For such a time as this" (Esther 4:14). In doing so, Holmes has been blessed with the "12 Point Action Plan Vision" highlighted in Chapter I of this book. Holmes believes this vision is achievable because, "with God, nothing is impossible" (Luke 1:37). Chapter II provides a presentations of key stakeholders committed to activate various components of the "12 Point Action Plan Vision." During the announcement of Rev. Holmes' candidacy at the National Press Club in Washington, D.C., these persons were in attendance and gave their presentations.

Chapter III of this book provides a summary of interviews of pastors across the country who share similar vision, ministries, and beliefs as Reverend Holmes. During the interviews, each pastor was asked: (1) What is your vision for the up-building and transformation of your community, (2) Why do you believe the Black church is relevant in the 21st century? (3) Why do you support Reverend Dr. R.B. Holmes Jr. for the presidency of the National Baptist Convention USA?

Chapter IV provides The Holmes Education Post's interview of Reverend Dr. R.B. Holmes, Jr. Thus, it is our hope that all Holmes references, credentials accolades and contributions to his family, church and community show that he is prepared spiritually, educationally, socially and physically to fulfill the needs of the convention with a strong vision and conviction.

1. Autobiography and "12 Point Action Plan Vision"

Autobiography

Reverend Dr. R. B. Holmes, Jr.
Pastor, Bethel Missionary Baptist Church
Tallahassee, Florida

Educational Preparation
- Central Florida Junior College (A.A.)
- Malone College, Canton, Ohio (B.A.)
- Methodist Theological Seminary,
- Delaware, Ohio (M.A.)
- Virginia Union University
- Richmond, VA (Doctor of Ministry)

The Ministry for God's Glory!
- Thirty-seven years in the ministry: Pastor of **First Timothy Baptist Church** of Jacksonville, FL, for 10 years (1976-1986)

- Presently, Pastor of **Bethel Missionary Baptist Church** for 27 years (1986-present) – one of the leading and largest churches in Florida with approximately 5,000 members

- Spiritual leader of forty **intergenerational, family-based**

ministries: *Christian Education, Music & Performing Arts, Infants, Children, Youth, Singles, Married Couples, Young Adults, Collegiates, Retirees, Military, Men's, Promise, Women's, Young Mothers Mentoring, Girl Scouts, Africare, Haiti, Homeless, Veterans Outreach, etc.*

- Founder and Executive Officer of **Bethel Christian Academy (1992); Steele-Collins Charter Middle School (1996); Steele-Collins All Male Charter Academy (2013); Bethel Family Restaurant (1996); Bethel Family Counselling Center (2006); Bethel Strip Mall (1996)**, etc.

- Led the Building of **Bethel Towers (2000)** providing housing for senior citizens; **Bethel Family Life Center (1999); Carolina Oaks Subdivision (2007); "Water Well"** in Caliquesse, Guinea Bissau, West Africa (1993); **Bethel Christian Academy II (The Bong Rong) in Mong Pong Village of the Ashanti Region, Ghana/West Africa (2007); Haiti Rehabilitation Facility, Pignon, Haiti**, for earthquake victims (2009)

- Significantly increased **Bethel's land acquisitions**, including the purchase of the **Wadsworth Property** in 2004 (approximately 3.5 acres) and the **"Bethel House" (1997)**, a project with Habitat for Humanity), etc.

Autobiography

Gubernatorial Appointments
- **Appointed by Governor Bob Graham:**
Florida Education Commission
- **Appointed by Governor Bob Martinez:**
Florida President, One Church, One Child
- **Appointed by Governor Jeb Bush:**
Judiciary Commission and Florida A&M University Board of Trustees
- **Appointed by Governor Charlie Crist:**
Florida A&M University Board of Trustees
- **Appointed by Governor Rick Scott**
Co-Chair, Task Force on Citizen Safety and Protection

Community Organizations
- Served on United Way Board of Directors
- Big Bend Hospice: Board of Directors
- Past National President: One Church-One Child
- NAACP & SCLC
- Alpha Phi Alpha Fraternity
- Past member of the Chamber of Commerce of Tallahassee, FL

Visionary Leader
- President and Founder of the **National Save the Family Now Movement, Inc.**

- Chairperson, **National Anti-Hazing/Anti-Violence Task Force**

- Chairperson, **Tallahassee Chapter, National Action Network**

- Past President of Region Two/Southeast of the **National Newspaper Publishers Association /NNPA** (includes the states of *Florida, Virginia, Mississippi, North Carolina, South Carolina, Tennessee, and Alabama*)

- Past- President of **the National Baptist Congress of Christian Education (1999-2009)**, an Auxiliary of the 7.5 million member National Baptist Convention, USA, Inc.

- **Member, Board of Trustees** for three Historically Black Colleges and Universities

  o Currently on the Board of Trustees of **Florida Memorial University**, Miami Gardens, Fl; **Edward Waters College**, Jacksonville, FL; **Malone University**, Canton, OH

  o Formerly served on the Board of Trustees of **Florida A&M University**, Tallahassee, FL, for eight years

Autobiography

- President and CEO of **Live Communications, Inc.** (Parent Company of the **Capital Outlook Newspaper**); Radio Station Owner of WTAL 1450 AM & WOCY FM 106.5 FM

Family Matters
- Son of the late Deacon and Mrs. R. B. (Lucille Johnson) Holmes, Sr.

- **Married to Dr. Gloria Price Holmes**

- Father of three; grandfather of three

- Author: The Private Christian School in the African American Church: It Is Needed

  Contributing Author: Marriage Matters: It's God's Will and Singles: Strengthened, Secured and Spirit-Filled

  www.betheltally.org

"12 POINT ACTION PLAN VISION"

Reverend Holmes has been a strong and dynamic leader of his church and community which all has led him to pursue the presidency of the National Baptist Convention. As we know, "all things work together for good to them that love God, to them who are called according to his purpose" (Romans 8:28). Holmes believes God is calling him for this purpose: "that he which hath begun a good work in you will perform it until the day of Jesus Christ" (Philippians 1:6). As such, the Lord has blessed Holmes to rebuild and reinvigorate the National Baptist Convention utilizing the following "12-Point Action Plan Vision."

1.
The National Baptist World Center Plan
We will create and develop a holistic model to transform The World Baptist Center into a full service ministry operation for supporting local Baptist churches and providing solutions to address the spiritual, social, educational and economic challenges of the 21st Century.

2.
The Pastors' Support Plan
We will provide support for pastors who have faithfully served the Convention for fifty or more years. These pastors will receive free housing at the annual sessions. Pastors who have real, proven needs will receive a quarterly stipend from the Convention.

3.
The Hotel Rebate and Lower Hotel Rates Plan
We will work to ensure that hotel rooms are affordable to all of our delegates. Pastors and lay persons who have faithfully served the Convention for forty years or more, will receive 15 percent or more room discount at annual sessions.

4.
The Save the Black Baptist Church Plan
We will work with churches to help them avoid foreclosure and bankruptcy. We will help churches to refinance their church mortgages by assisting them in getting the lowest possible interest rates available. We will help small congregations and churches survive.

"12 POINT ACTION PLAN VISION"

5. **The NBC, USA, Inc. Outreach and Inreach Evangelistic Plan**
We will own television and radio stations in order to provide opportunities for our young and seasoned pastors, preachers and teachers to be heard and viewed on the world-wide web and all social and electronic media.

6. **The Financial Stability and Stewardship Plan**
We will develop the NBC, USA, Inc. Credit Union. We must have our own monetary resources to help our churches and our membership. Many other religious denominations and groups have their own credit unions. We must organize strong African-American fiscal institutions.

7. **The Church Development Ministry Plan**
We will develop a plan that will help local churches to develop homes for the elderly, academies for our students, veteran services, substance abuse retreat sites, couples, singles, youth, young adults, children, senior citizens and other family-based ministries.

8. **The Christian Educational Plan**
We will develop relevant Christian Education programs that will be the best in the country. We must encourage churches to support our Sunday School Publishing Board. We must continue to provide quality literature and materials for local churches.

9. **The Urban and Rural Community Development Plan**
We will target several urban and rural cities with a strategic plan that will create job training programs, faith-based schools, retirement homes, homes for first-time homeowners, grocery stores, mental health clinics/hospitals and financial institutions. We will work to save Black-owned farms.

"12 POINT ACTION PLAN VISION"

10.
The Community Empowerment and Engagement Plan
We will cultivate a plan of action to save, sustain and strengthen Historically Black Colleges and Universities. We will network with civil rights groups and social justice organizations to challenge policies, procedures and people who try to turn back our hard earned civil and human rights.

11.
The Professional Sports Plan
We will partner with the National Football League, Major League Baseball and the National Basketball Association to develop character building programs for athletes. We will develop a model for building moral strength, Biblical stewardship principles and helping athletes to become Godly role models for our young people. Also, we will use young pastors as chaplains for these professional teams.

12.
The Young Pastors, Ministers and Young Adult Plan
We will develop opportunities for young pastors and ministers to participate in the life of the Convention and to use their skills and gifts for the strengthening of the Convention. We will forge an aggressive master plan to reach, train and retain young people in local Baptist churches.

2. Key Stakeholders Presentations of Action Plan

Evangelism

Jesus taught in Matthew 9:37-38 that prayer for laborers was absolutely foundational and necessary in order to cultivate the hearts of the redeemed to reach out with the message of Jesus to those who are unreached. Jesus included in His prayer for His followers, a prayer for unity, indicating unity among God's people is absolutely essential to effective evangelism (John 17:20-21). Jesus' disciples labored in prayer in the Upper Room before they began to share the Gospel of Jesus in Jerusalem, Judea and Samaria (Acts 1:8; 13-14).

The following initiatives will undergird Dr. R. B. Holmes' 20/20 Action Vision Plan for Evangelism:

1. The National Baptist Convention Day of Prayer for Evangelistic Empowerment and Effectiveness to be established and held each year on whatever day in May that Pentecost Sunday falls on (Matthew 9:37-38; John 17:20-21).

2. The National Baptist Convention Gospel of the Kingdom Evangelism Tract. We will produce an evangelism tract that focuses on the gospel as preached by Jesus and His Disciples, to be made available to all National Baptist Convention Churches, as a tool to share the gospel. We will offer training opportunities to all pastors and church leaders regarding the most effective ways to utilize this tract. We plan to assimilate and distribute this tract to wherever people are gathered as a witness to our Lord Jesus Christ (Luke 4:43).

3. The National Baptist Convention Growth Through the Sunday School Evangelism Plan. We believe that evangelism and discipleship are inextricably combined. We will encourage and train Sunday School leaders/teachers on how to utilize Sunday School units as a tool for evangelism (Matthew 28:19).

4. The National Baptist Convention Evangelistic Church Planting Initiative. Church plants are often more effective in reaching new souls for Christ and expanding the Kingdom than existing churches. Where NBC churches are few and far in-between, we propose to plant and establish new churches whose focus will be evangelism, discipleship, exaltation and the elevation of society. Thus, we will fulfill the mandate of Jesus to be the salt of the earth, the light of the world and a city sitting upon a hill (Acts 13:1-3).

5. The National Baptist Convention Evangelism/Discipleship Training Regional Celebrations. We propose to conduct regional evangelism/discipleship training celebration rallies in strategic locations throughout America to equip believers to evangelize and to be rooted and grounded (edified) in their faith. In these evangelism/discipleship rallies we will challenge and equip men, women and youth to grow in their faith and share their faith with those who have not yet come to faith in Christ (Colossians 2:6-7).

Reverend Dr. Wm. Dwight McKissic, Sr., Pastor
Cornerstone Baptist Church, Arlington, Texas

Education

Having a quality education is vital to the stability of our economy. It enables individuals to gain employment and contributes to the U.S. tax base. Yet, only one third of African American students finish high school. This contributes to the unemployment rate for high school dropouts of 12.4 percent compared to 8.3 percent for high school graduates and 6.2 percent for college graduates with a four-year degree.

We know that many African American students and other minorities are confronted with challenges at home and the community that inhibits them from coming to school ready to learn. At the same time, we advocate the need to prepare our students for 21st century skills, but we do not have the educational resources in many of our schools to personalize instruction for African American students. In fact, our educational system is outdated and not equipped to address appropriately the learning styles, abilities and behaviors of these students.

As the National Superintendent of Education for the National Save the Family Now Movement, Inc. and the presidential campaign of Reverend Dr. R.B. Holmes Jr. for the National Baptist Convention USA, we propose researched-based educational resources and programs to support African American students and other minorities who are having a difficult time in obtaining a quality education. Some of these initiatives include (1) a partnership with Historical Black Colleges and Private Universities to establish five elementary and secondary schools; (2) a partnership with African American churches to establish private schools in 25 cities, (3) a partnership with government officials to establish an all male and female boarding schools; (4) a partnership with the GED Testing Service to assist dropout students in completing all the requirements for graduation and (5) a partnership with community colleges to establish Industry Certification programs on the premises of African American churches.

We will use the research of The Holmes Education Post to stay abreast of current issues and best practices in education. We will enlist the support of public and private foundations to fund these initiatives in an effort to "save" our families and communities, pay our contribution to the work that is needed to strengthen, sustain and revitalize our communities and foster growth and productivity to our economy. Annually, 1.2 million students dropout of high school resulting in a 1.8 billion loss in tax revenue. There are about 4 million unfilled jobs in the U.S. due to the lack of adequate education and training of applicants for the workforce. As we invest in African American students and other minorities, we can offset unnecessary U.S. spending by affording our students the knowledge and skills to transition into these jobs. Consequently, these students will become tax contributors and boost our nation's economy.

Ronald W. Holmes, Ph.D.
National Superintendent of Education
National Save the Family Now Movement, Inc.

Education

I, Dr. Cullian W. Hill, am disturbed concerning the lack of education among our Black children. Over the past ten years, there has been a decline in graduation of high school and college students. Many of our parents are not seriously involved in their children's performance at school. Many of them do not get their children to school on time. The children's attendance at school is a serious problem, meaning they miss twenty to forty days a year during the school year. Many will not attend parent-teacher conferences and other major parent involvement activities.

We, as a Convention must address this problem and seek alternatives to address this problem across this nation. We, as a Convention must organize quality charter schools across the country with pastors and other groups that will improve and impact our communities and the lives of children.

Dr. R. B. Holmes has given leadership in the educational arena and is a proponent of educational improvement. For over two decades, he has given of his resources and time to make sure boys and girls get a quality education.

One of my reasons for joining his ticket is that he is very involved with children. At Commonwealth Community Development Academy, of which I am the founder and CEO for the last eighteen years, along with my late wife Mrs. Lucille Hill, I have devoted much of my life and resources in educating children in reading, math, science and technology. Education will be at the top of our goals.

Dr. Cullian W. Hill, Pastor of Greater Concord Missionary Baptist Church
Detroit, Michigan

Economic Development

Winning the future for cities and metropolitan areas is part of Rev. Dr. R.B. Holmes, Jr. "12 Point Action Plan for the Rebuilding and Reinvigoration of The National Baptist Convention USA, Inc." Isaiah 61:4 gives us a picture of what a great church should look like. They will rebuild the ancient ruins and restore places that were long devastated. They will renew places that were broken and lost and people will be rebuilt, restored and renewed to become fully committed disciples of Jesus Christ who will then rebuild, restore and renew the world around them.

Having emerged from the worst recession in generations, Rev. Dr. R.B. Holmes, Jr. has put forward a plan to rebuild our churches, our cities, our metropolitan neighborhoods and our communities and win the future by out-innovating, out-educating and out-building our global competitors and creating the jobs, housing and industries of tomorrow. But the NBCUSA, Inc. cannot rebuild our financial infrastructure and win the future if we pass on a mountain of debt to our state-wide churches, pastors and memberships. We must restore fiscal responsibility and reform NBCUSA, Inc. to make it more effective, efficient and open to its membership.

Reverend Dr. R.B. Holmes, Jr.'s "12 Point Action Plan Vision" for the rebuilding and reinvigoration of NBCUSA, Inc. is a responsible approach that puts the NBCUSA, Inc. on a path to live within its means so it can invest in its future by cutting wasteful spending and making tough choices on some things. It cannot afford while keeping the investments it needs to grow NBCUSA, Inc. and create housing, jobs and greater economic development opportunities for its membership churches. Rev. Dr. R.B. Holmes, Jr.'s "12 Point Action Plan Vision" (a) spurs job creation and supports strong economic growth; (b) supports creating a NBCUSA, Inc. credit union which will support business growth and lending in low income and minority communities; (c) provides small business access to credit and technical assistance; (d) establishes a national infrastructure credit union that would operate like a national bank; (e) improves the condition membership churches whose infrastructure is under great need of repair or need to be rebuilt; (f) invests in regional and national community planning efforts for sustainable development; (g) expands access to and improve adoption of broadband high speed, wireless broadband which is fast becoming a critical component of business operations and economic growth; (h) assists NBCUSA, Inc. members in applying for community development block grants programs that would revitalize distressed urban neighborhoods; (i) promotes affordable homeownership and help families stay in their homes; (j) assists member churches find critical funding for health centers; (k) prevents hunger and improves nutrition; (l) preserves affordable pre senior rental opportunities and (m) expands the promise neighborhood program to prepare more students for college.

These are just a few of Rev. Dr. R.B. Holmes, Jr. vibrant, diverse and exciting visions he has for the rebuilding and reinvigoration of the National Baptist Convention USA, Inc.

Rev. Jonas Milton, Associate Minister
First Timothy Missionary Baptist Church
Jacksonville, Florida

Renewable Energy and Preservation Plan

During his 2013 State of the Union Address, President Obama announced a bold challenge to the country:

1. To double the energy productivity of the U.S. economy by 2030

2. To generate 80 percent of the country's electricity from a diverse set of clean renewable energy sources like wind, solar, biomass, hydropower; nuclear power; efficient natural gas; and clean coal by 2035.

The President has taken several steps to improve the Federal Government's productivity and has committed billions of dollars through private sector contracting to reduce the energy and carbon intensity of federal buildings throughout the country, at no cost to tax payers.

Continued financial commitments and a national Clean Energy Standard (CES) will provide the signal investors need to move billions of dollars of capital off the sidelines and into the clean energy economy, creating jobs, reducing air pollution and greenhouse gas emissions and making America more competitive in the 21st century.

It is my belief, that as we continue to increase our policy and financial commitments to the clean energy economy, a coherent vision needs to emerge that includes the full participation of underrepresented communities in these contracting opportunities, as well as helps our urban cities transform to sustainable green communities. This vision must extend across multiple federal agencies and private sector companies.

The success of a clean energy economy relies on our human resource capital. This is why it is also critical that we prepare students of all age groups for this new economy. Our students must have a strong foundation in science, technology, engineering and mathematics also known as STEM. This commitment will generate the scientists, engineers, and mathematicians necessary to generate new ideas, new products, and entirely new industries.

African Americans, Hispanics, Native Americans, and women are seriously underrepresented in many STEM fields, thus depriving the nation of the full benefit of their talents and unique perspectives. The vision for clean energy must include opportunities for expanding their participation.

The health and vibrancy of our communities depends on embracing new green technologies, practices and educational opportunities. It is imperative that underrepresented communities become an integral participant across the many sectors of the clean energy economy.

Al Morten
Advisor to Dr. R.B. Holmes on Renewable Energy and Preservation

Social Justice

We are living in complex, challenging times and our community is being impacted in troubling and some unprecedented ways. It is imperative that we marshal our efforts and resources as a community in order to evolve as a stronger unit and a firm foundation upon which generations yet born must stand. We must all be, "Drum Majors for Justice."

We are painfully aware of the fact that we are burying our children due to unthinkable situations. Therefore, we will be calling for the country to reconsider Stand Your Ground Laws across this nation, as well as, to provide safe zones for our children to not just survive, but to thrive and soar. We are losing too many people in our community due to violence and indifference. We will address a wide range of issues and call for the support of important initiatives including but not limited to:

1. Support of the Affordable Health Care Act and the expansion of Medicaid;

2. Support of President Obama's "My Brother's Keeper" Initiative;

3. Support of an increase in the minimum wage;

4. Support of the. US Attorney General's initiative to restore voting privileges to convicted felons who have served their time in prison;

5. Development and implementation of anti-hazing programs and policies on our college and university campuses; and

6. Support of efforts to end all voter suppression.

We are determined to lift our community and all of America to higher ground.

Judge Glenda Hatchett
Advisor to Rev. Dr. Holmes in the areas of Social and Legal Justice

Social Justice

In 1960, I was five years old and went to school and was placed in kindergarten. I can distinctively remember every morning before class, my teacher instructed each student to stand and place their right hand over their chest, look at a red, white, and blue flag, then repeat these words, "I pledge allegiance to the flag of the United States of America, and to the republic for which it stands, one Nation under God, indivisible, with liberty and justice for all." I was told we live in the greatest society in the world because we believe in social justice. We believe in promoting a just society by challenging injustice and valuing diversity.

Social Justice exists when all people share a common humanity and, therefore, have a right to equitable treatment, support for human rights and a fair allocation of community resources. In America, citizens are not supposed to be discriminated against, nor their welfare and well-being constrained or prejudiced on the basis of gender, sexuality, religion, political affiliations, age, race, disability, social class or socioeconomic circumstances. Unfortunately, some laws are created in America that can be used in a discriminatory and prejudicial manner. I believe the "Stand Your Ground" laws have been used to discriminate and promote prejudice.

Trayvon Martin had a civil right to walk home with candy and ice tea in his hand without being killed. Jordan Davis had a civil right to sit in a SUV and listen to music without being shot to death. Americans must continue to challenge, repeal, reform or replace these laws. We can only have true social justice, when all people have a right to equitable treatment.

Reverend Dr. Leonard T. King
Pastor of the First Zion Baptist Church - Cleveland, Ohio

Robert D. Champion Drum Major for Change Foundation, Inc.

A Haze Ending Foundation Deeply Rooted in God

The following are our vision, mission, goals and objectives for the Robert D. Champion Drum Major for Change Foundation, Inc. The vision is to eradicate hazing nationwide. The mission is to create awareness of the culture of hazing and eliminate the mentality that has influenced countless individuals into the hazing lifestyle. The goals and objectives are to educate the community on the effects of hazing; prevent further casualties caused by the practice of hazing; provide empowerment initiatives geared towards public awareness; present potential solutions to stamp out the custom of hazing and define and identify the meaning of hazing.

Mr. & Mrs. Robert Champion Sr.

The Trayvon Martin Foundation

The Trayvon Martin Foundation was established by Sybrina Fulton and Tracy Martin in March 2012 as a not-for-profit organization under the auspices of the Miami Foundation. The Foundation's purpose is to create awareness of how violent crime impacts the families of the victims and to provide support and advocacy for those families in response to the murder of Trayvon Martin. The scope of the Foundation's mission is to advocate that crime victims and their families are not ignored in the discussions about violent crime, to increase public awareness of all forms of racial ethnic and gender profiling, to educate youth on conflict resolution techniques and to reduce the incidences where confrontations between strangers turn deadly.

Sybrina Fulton and Tracy Martin

Support Our Veterans

We need a "spiritual" draft as the National Baptist Convention, USA, Inc., declares war with a clear mission in mind. We are calling on the young, and the aged veterans and non-veterans to join us in fighting the war against crime and injustice, illiteracy, poverty, homelessness, substandard housing, health deterioration, mental weakness, economic instability, and living in despair. We are calling on every pastor, every church body, and every church member in the NBC, USA, Inc. to identify every veteran and every person that lacks the skills to become a productive citizen of this great country.

Let us develop skills training in brick masonry, plumbing, carpentry, electrical wiring, culinary arts, and auto maintenance, to name just a few. These skills are marketable and can lift those stuck in despair in this land of plenty. The economic crisis has crippled job opportunities for many of our veterans and our young people. We witness veterans sitting by the roads and on our streets begging for food and asking for work, with many sleeping under bridges. Such undeserving acts in this land of opportunity that they fought to ensure liberty and justice for all epitomize shame that is not indicative of Christians and true Americans.

We see many of our young children caught up in the criminal justice system that seems to be a revolving door. Yes, the NBC, USA, Inc. and our vast membership declares "spiritual" war on a continuance of such blatant and shameful acts and we will use all of our God given talents to ensure a quick and decisive end to such malady. We are our brother's keeper and the blood of Jesus Christ covers us when we walk and act in his will.

Reverend Dr. Thurman B. Everett, Pastor
Bryant Swamp Missionary Baptist Church
Bladenboro, North Carolina

Health Care

The World Health Organization defines health as "a state of complete physical, mental and social well-being and not merely the absence of disease or infirmity." The goals of the healthcare arm of Dr. R. B. Holmes' Action Plan would include:

- Improve access to affordable, patient-centered healthcare for all, especially those who are disenfranchised.

- Improve statistics by decreasing health disparities.

- Improve the pipeline of minority physicians through mentoring and scholarships.

- Mobilize physicians in our ranks to devote volunteer hours to the communities most in need, thereby bringing the healthcare to the people. This would hopefully expand to the point of having healthcare facilities and even hospitals.

Special areas of focus would include cardiovascular disease, diabetes, cancer, obesity, and mental health.

Cyneetha Strong, MD - Family Physician
Tallahassee, Florida

Health Care

Mental health issues often go unnoticed until someone brings it to your attention whether it's a loved one, pastor or professional. Often individuals are not receptive to seeking help due to the stigma that has been placed on mental health. Many people who would benefit from mental health services opt not to pursue them or fail to fully participate once they have begun. One of the primary reasons for this disengagement is stigma; namely, to avoid the label of mental illness and the harm it brings, people decide not to seek or fully participate in treatment. Stigma diminishes self-esteem and robs people of social opportunities.

Researchers have found that minorities in the United States receive fewer mental health services than whites. This analysis compares rates of outpatient mental health treatment according to race and ethnicity using more recent, population-based data, from the 1997 National Ambulatory Medical Care Survey and National Hospital Ambulatory Medical Care Survey. In the primary care setting, Hispanics and Blacks had lower visit rates (per 1,000 population) for drug therapy than whites (48.3 and 73.7 vs. 109.0; $P < .0001$ and $P < .01$, respectively). Blacks also had a lower visit rate for talk therapy (mental health counseling or psychotherapy) than whites (23.6 vs. 42.5; $P < .01$). In the psychiatric setting, Hispanics and Blacks had lower visit rates than whites for talk therapy (38.4 and 33.6 vs. 85.1; $P < .0001$ for both comparisons) and drug therapy (38.3 and 29.1 vs. 71.8; $P < .0001$ for both comparisons). These results indicate that minorities receive about half as much outpatient mental health care as whites. It is our duty to educate our constituents on these illnesses in order to bridge the gap between mental illness and treatment.

Dr. Tolonda Tate/Executive Director of Bethel Family Counseling and Outreach Center
Tallahassee, Florida

Save the Family Now – The Purpose

Under the leadership of our founder and president, Reverend Dr. R. B. Holmes, Jr., the purpose of the National Save the Family Now Movement is to save, strengthen, and sustain the Black family in particular and all families in general. Dr. Holmes has been leading the Movement, which is now part of his presidential platform, to:

- Develop a 2020 Strategic Plan that will clearly outline policies and programs that champion the family while concurrently advocating the demise of activities that denigrate and or demean families.

- Develop a positive, proactive agenda for holistic programs, events and activities that will rebuild, reenergize and stimulate the family structure.

There is a correlation between the rise in broken and dysfunctional families and the rise in the incidence of social maladies. There is an inalienable link between the way our families go and the way society goes. Family erosion cannot be divorced from public and fiscal policy.

The biggest economic problem in America may be the breakdown of the American family. According to the Census Bureau, in 2010, in households with children that had married parents, 8.4 percent lived in poverty. In households with children headed by a single mother, 39.6 percent lived in poverty. Stable marriages and families contribute to economic stability and prosperity. President Obama's fatherhood initiative encourages local communities to strengthen our nation's families. His "My Brother's Keeper" initiative identifies the challenge of ensuring success for young men of color as a "moral issue for our country." He cited statistics showing that Black boys are more likely to be suspended from school, less likely to be able to read, and almost certain to encounter the criminal justice system as either a perpetrator or a victim.

The Reverend Dr. R. B. Holmes, Jr., 2014 candidate for President of the National Baptist Convention, USA, Inc., has outlined in his 12 Point Action Plan campaign platform a vision designed to serve as a roadmap to lead the Convention in holistically addressing and meeting the needs of families in our churches and communities. His platform entails, among other things,

- Utilizing the Convention's collective resources to implement and develop community-based programs and solutions designed to enhance the spiritual, physical, social and economic well-being of our people.

- Networking, empowering and mobilizing National Baptists to rise to another level in addressing the complex and often controversial moral and social issues of our day.

Reverend Dr. John H. Grant, Pastor
Mt. Zion Missionary Baptist Church, Inc.
Asheville, North Carolina

Save the Family Now – The Black Male

Our Black family is in crisis and moral decay. If we are going to restore the family, we must first reclaim and revitalize the Black male, reconcile the Black father to his home and children, then intentionally invest in the life of the Black boy. Outlined are four transformational proof-positive initiatives to do just that.

The first initiative is to reaffirm and nurture the positive self, spiritual and cultural identity of the Black male. If we want to see family restoration, it's imperative for the Black male to have a personal transformation. This foundational principle is paramount to reclaiming the Black male. Instituting customized life planning and goal setting, self-awareness and affirmation exercises, theme focused interactive specialized training undergirded with biblical truths and prayer ensures male revitalization and strengthening of the family unit.

The second initiative is to build and promote positive and healthy relationships. When we provide and cultivate effective mentoring, authentic accountability, skillful role modeling, and address and heal life wounds through life-altering programming in male focused community, we will see viable change in the lives of Black men and boys, reconciliation of relationships and reconnection of fathers to their children.

The third initiative is to promote and cultivate leadership empowerment in Black males and youth. Modeling effective leadership skills and practice, defining and assigning leadership roles through concentrated training, and instilling and promoting effective leadership skills and roles from childhood to manhood empowers Black males to know and take their rightful position in the home, church and community.

The last initiative is to foster and implement character development. When character traits are properly taught and caught in young boys and men through innovative workshops, transformational curriculum, positive Black male exposure, organizational recreation, purposeful activities, intensive boot camps, and prayer, we will see vast improvements in our families. Implementation of these four transformative initiatives to reclaim and revitalize the Black male will be efficacious to "Save Our Family Now."

Dr. Darryl K. Webster, Senior Pastor and Men's BOOTCAMP Founder
Emmanuel Missionary Baptist Church; Indianapolis, Indiana

Save the Family Now – The Community

The very reason for restoring and reviving inner cities and rural communities is for the benefit, strengthening, and protection of the children and families who reside there. We at Casey Family Programs, the Nation's largest operating foundation focused on safely reducing the need for foster care and building communities of hope, believe the example that Rev. Holmes and the Bethel Missionary Baptist Church family have created in Tallahassee offers a roadmap for other communities to do likewise. That is why we chose to partner with Bethel to support and lift up their story as a beacon of hope and vision for others to 'come and see'.

Casey Family programs believes that a community of hope like that created by Pastor Holmes and his congregation is indeed keeping more children safely in their homes...with stronger families able to provide for their well-being...and that with leadership, commitment, and a shining example like Bethel, this good news can be taken all across our Great Nation. We see R.B. Holmes as an inspired leader who can do just that. And we stand ready to partner with him and others with this hopeful vision for children and families.

Page B. Walley, Ph.D. - Casey Family Programs
Managing Director, Strategic Consulting - Auburn, Alabama

Save the Family Now – The Bowl

Historically, Black Colleges and Universities (HBCU) have a proud tradition of Football. Visionary leadership from the likes of Eddie Robinson, Jake Gaither, and John Merritt wanted to showcase HBCU students on the highest of platforms. These coaches took their teams far west to play in the likes of the Rose Bowl, as far south as the Cotton Bowl, and up North playing in the Meadowlands (Giant Stadium). It was important that student athletes knew they could compete in the biggest of venues in sports but also in life.

In the 1990's and early 2000's, the HBCU had two Bowl games that celebrated the best in Black College Football. The Heritage Bowl (MEAC vs. SWAC) and The Pioneer Bowl (SIAC vs. CIAA) were both played at the Georgia Dome, and were a huge success. These events consisted of great competiveness between the teams, electrifying atmosphere, great tailgating, and awesome band exhibitions. Unfortunately, these games lost sponsorship and the events were cancelled.

The vision that has been researched and expressed is to bring these quality games back to the forefront of Black College Football. The "Save the Family" Bowl (MEAC vs. SWAC) (SIAC vs. CIAA) will have the same format as the Heritage and Pioneer Bowl. The first game will be The MEAC vs. SWAC at 1:30p.m., and the second game will be the SIAC vs. CIAA at 6:00p.m. The games will take place a week before Christmas. The teams should all be in Atlanta by 5:00p.m., Thursday night. There will be a banquet Friday night before Saturday's game. The banquet hall should house four teams. The banquet should consist of a keynote speaker, dinner, and awards for the top scholar of each team. Academics is praised before athletics. The teams will also need police escorts to the actual stadium, and meals after the game (Popeye's or KFC). The winners of each game will be presented with the Dr. Holmes Trophy of Excellence immediately after the game.

This game will not only honor the great football being played in the present but also expose youth to College and Universities for future investments. The games, while competitive, will shed a sence of pride among all that take part. The winner of each game will share a portion of revenue generated and all participants should realize a

Revitalizing the National Baptist Convention, USA, Inc.

recognition amount. Follow-up discussions will exact the payout amounts to each university. We hope that you all will share in the Vision.

Coach Joseph D. Taylor, Director of Athletics
Virginia Union University

3. Interviews by Supporting Pastors

Reverend Tommie L. Brewer
Gethsemane Baptist Church
Canton, Ohio

Gethsemane Baptist Church is located in Canton, Ohio. The church has been in existence for 58 years. It currently operates under the leadership of Reverend Tommie L. Brewer who has served as the pastor for the past five years.

What is your vision for the up-building and transformation of your community?

My vision is to reach as many people as possible and show love through an outreach ministry and street ministry. Every fourth Saturday, for example, we provide free lunches to people throughout the City of Canton. My vision is also to minimize the violence occurring in the City of Canton. I believe that one of the things missing in the community is love for one another. We have to instill love for one another back in the community.

Why do you believe the Black church is relevant in the 21st century?

The Black church is relevant because people are more into the word of God. People are beginning to be more word driven and less emotional driven. Word driven people are seeking more knowledge from the teaching of the word of God. People are not just accepting what pastors are telling them such as what they can or can't do if the message does not pertain to the word of God. People are not just taking a no for an answer when the message is not in God's plan. If the message is in God's plan for our life, that's what people are seeking in this century.

Why do you support Reverend Dr. R.B. Holmes Jr. for the presidency of the National Baptist Convention USA?

First, I believe that Reverend R.B. Holmes' word is his bond. From my observation, I see that the Lord is in him and with him. Reverend Holmes is a very knowledgeable and educated person with the passion for love to all humankind. Reverend Holmes

43

and I gained training under the late Reverend W. C. Henderson of Antioch Baptist Church in Canton, Ohio. During this time, Reverend Holmes followed Reverend Henderson everywhere such as to the nursing home, hospital and the street community. I heard Reverend Holmes say one time, "If you do good to your people, they would do good to you." So that let me know that he is a man who was not concerned about what someone else could do for him but what he could do for people. That is why I support him.

Reverend Dr. Thurman B. Everett
Bryant Swamp Missionary Baptist Church
Bladenboro, North Carolina.

Bryant Swamp Missionary Baptist Church is located in Bladenboro, North Carolina. The church was founded July 1871, and has been in existence for 143 years. Reverend Dr. Thurman B. Everett has served as the pastor for the past 18 years.

What is your vision for the up-building and transformation of your community?

The up-building and transformation of our community requires programs of hope: spiritual, mental, and material. Many of our people are suffering from despair, hopelessness, discouragement, desperation and depression. To counter these conditions, we must continue to offer the word of God to meet the spiritual and mental needs. One of the greatest needs is the plight of substandard housing. To address this need, we will offer skills training in carpentry, plumbing, electrical wiring, basic computer training, brick laying and cooking. Once the required skills are obtained, contact teams should be employed to go into depressed and blighted areas and do rehabilitation by bringing homes up to a decent living standard. I believe the whole community will be uplifted.

Why do you believe the Black church is relevant in the 21st century?

The Black church is very relevant in the 21st century because it is the only living body that can speak truth to power without reservation or intimidation. The church must speak to every wrong, false, inappropriate, illegal, immoral and unethical practice in our society; then demonstrate truth in every walk of life. The Black church must be Christ centered and not world centered. We must take Jesus Christ to the world and not allow the world to take over the church. When the church keeps its focus on Christ Jesus, people will hear the message and incrementally change over time. When the Black church speaks the truth, we must also teach our people our history on a regular basis. When our people know the truth, "The truth will set us free;" and cause esprit-de-corps, a spirit of devotion and enthusiasm to set in.

Why do you support Reverend Dr. R.B. Holmes Jr. for the presidency of the National Baptist Convention USA?

I support Dr. R.B. Holmes Jr. for president of the National Baptist Convention USA. I believe he is called by God, ordained by God and set apart by God for such a time as this. My belief is he is the most qualified to fill the position of the presidency of the NBCUSA. I have found him to be a man of impeccable character, forward vision, steadfast spirit and a genuine love for God and mankind.

Reverend Dr. John H. Grant
Mt. Zion Missionary Baptist Church of Asheville, Inc.

The Mt. Zion Missionary Baptist Church (MZMBC) of Asheville, Inc. is located in the Blue Ridge Mountains of Western North Carolina in the Central Business District of downtown Asheville, North Carolina. Reverend Dr. John Grant has served as pastor of MZMBC since 1989. The purpose of Mt. Zion is to worship God, make disciples and minister to the needs of the whole person, locally, nationally and internationally based on Psalm 100, 150; Matthew 28:18-20; Luke 4:18-19; John 3:16 and Acts 1:8.

What is your vision for the up-building and transformation of your community?

The central thrust of my vision is preaching, teaching, and witnessing to the gospel of our Lord and Savior Jesus the Christ which we do daily. Understood holistically, this commitment to Christ has been the main motivation for the organization in 1997 of the Mt. Zion Community Development, Inc. ("MZCD"), one of the signature accomplishments of my vision for up-building and transforming our community. This is a 501(C) (3) non-profit, for which I served as founding president and chief executive officer. With four staff positions, since its inception in 1997, MZCD has operated four widely acclaimed programs:

- Project Nurturing Asheville and Area Families ("NAF") – working to help African American women have healthy babies and reduce the minority infant mortality rate

- Teen Pregnancy Prevention Initiative ("TPPI") – working to reduce the rate of teen pregnancies

- The Elizabeth Grant Hill Campus of Learners: Center for Health, Technology, and Entrepreneurship — working to bridge the digital divide in our communities

- Real Estate Development for housing, office, retail — working to provide economic opportunities and eliminate blight

MZCD has raised and invested millions of dollars for its community projects, as well as provided part and full-time jobs with full-time benefits, including medical insurance, retirement, etc. Project NAF has been cited in Asheville as a national model and showcased nationally. The Elizabeth Grant Hill Campus of Learners was made possible by the generosity of Dr. Grant's cousins – former NFL great Calvin Hill and wife Janet; and former NBA All-Star Grant Hill and his wife, R&B recording Star Tamia. Campus of Learners was cited as the "2001 Faith-Based Initiative of the Year" by the North Carolina Association of Community Development Corporations.

Another signature accomplishment of my Christ-centered vision for up-building and transforming our community was the organization of the Eagle-Market Streets Development Corporation, a 501(C) (3) non-profit, where I served as founding president, chairman, and chief executive officer. This corporation has already begun construction of Eagle Market Place, a $12 million project which will provide 62 affordable/workforce apartments, over 6,000 square feet of community and neighborhood space, and almost 7,000 square feet of commercial, retail, and office space. Visit info@mtnhousing.org for more details on the project. The Corporation's official website is www.eaglemarketsts.net.

My vision has been focused on empowering our community with self-help tools. In addition to MZCD and the Eagle-Market Streets non-profits, I have been involved in organizing two other non-profit corporations since coming to Asheville in 1989.

We have also emphasized teaching parishioners and others not only to work for money, but to make money work for them. Thus we have taught classes on money management, debt-free living, investments, setting up endowment funds, etc.

My vision has been to lead the church in exemplifying what we teach. For example, in the mid 1990's, I led the church to purchase three adjacent properties as an investment for a future mixed-use development for housing, office, administrative, retail, and supportive services. To date, the church has invested approximately six hundred thousand dollars in these properties. However, those same properties were appraised in June of 2013 for $4 million. Also, because of location, location, location (as they say in real estate), several developers have made offers to either purchase the properties or join the church in a joint-venture development partnership.

Each of the initiatives just mentioned is anchored in the church and addresses the spiritual, physical, emotional, and financial health of families. The acronym "T.E.A.C.H" summarizes my vision for the up-building and transformation of our community:

> **T** = Teach and Train to Provide Tools with the goal of
> **E** = Educating, Equipping and Empowering so that persons can become
> **A** = Advocates for the good of themselves and others, and
> **C** = Not be merely Consumers but Contributors who make
> **H** = Healthy lifestyle choices, spiritually, physically, emotionally, socially, and financially.

Why do you believe the Black church is relevant in the 21st century?

One of many reasons the Black church is and will remain relevant in the 21st century is that of the particularities of the Black experience. I am referencing the uniqueness or "specialty" which has characterized, and still characterizes the Sitz im Leben (situation in life) of Blacks in the American and/or New World context from the time of the Middle Passage to the present. "Specialty," as certain historians have pointed out, does not mean better than or inferior to others, it means particularity, a difference born out the unique experiences through which Blacks have passed and continue to pass in this country.

To the extent this difference persists into the 21st century, and I'm not aware of any evidence suggesting that it has not or will not, to that extent the Black church will remain relevant. In every segment of society, the special status of Blacks persists. Whether one looks at education, economics, health, housing, etc., the disparities which exist for Blacks and other minorities are well documented. It remains true to this day that in virtually every category one looks, Blacks generally are worse off. Numerous studies and statistics corroborate this unfortunate reality.

Throughout America's history, from slavery to Jim Crow to integration, the Black church played vital roles in the upward mobility of Black America. Historically, the

Black church has been poised to address the special status of Black people in ways that are unique from any other institution in the Black or White community. As the Reverend Dr. Charles Adams put it in a sermon, I heard at Hampton University Minister's Conference:

The church – inspired, empowered and equipped by the Risen Savior – is all we own and control. It's the preserver of our culture. It's the producer of our genius. It's the power base for our political ascendancy. It's the parent of our music and art. It's the sponsor of our creativity, versatility and ingenuity. It is the incubator for our leadership. It is the storehouse for the disinherited. It is the power base for the disfranchised. It is a hospital for wounded souls. It is a love tabernacle for the hated and exploited. It is an open door to the least, the lost, the unlucky and the left out. It is the biggest enemy to the status quo. It is a cultural agency for anti-defamation. It is a rock in a weary land. It is a shelter from a stormy blast of bigotry. It faces a frowning world and says, "We Shall Overcome!"

Some contend that the Black church is outdated, irrelevant, and obsolete. Those who make such contentions, in my observation, are usually those not involved in any church and are particularly ignorant of the history and role the Black church has played, and continues to play, in the history and uplift of our people.

Why do you support Reverend Dr. R.B. Holmes Jr. for the presidency of the National Baptist Convention USA?

The great commandment to love our neighbors as ourselves (Matthew 22:39, Mark 12:31, Luke 10:27) means to be concerned for their total welfare, the good of their souls, their bodies and their communities. As a pastor of forty years and a denominational leader for most of those years, I can say unequivocally that the life and ministry of Dr. R. B. Holmes, Jr. exemplify a passionate, competent and consecrated dedication to the total welfare of persons. Consider the following:

- His 27 year ministry at the Bethel Church and the Casey Foundation's designation of the Bethel Model as a "Community of Hope" for the saving, strengthening and sustaining of families;

- 10 year tenure as President of the National Baptist Congress of Christian Education;

- Entrepreneur and owner of Tallahassee's Capital Outlook Newspaper and Radio Station WTAL 1450 AM and WOCY 106 FM, showing his understanding of the importance of having media we own for the dissemination of pertinent information for the uplift of our communities;

- Founder and President of the National Save the Family Now Movement, Inc., which now has chapters in a number of cities in America, including the city of Asheville, NC. (www.savethefamilynow.com);

- His 12 Point Action Plan Vision for the rebuilding and reinvigoration of NBC, USA. (www.gobig4holmes2014.org)

His overall ministry provides best practice models (not impracticable theories) for holistic ministries that can be utilized not only to rebuild and reinvigorate the National Baptist Convention, USA, Inc., but also communities across America and beyond. For Dr. Holmes, performance and positive results are a matter of record and due largely to his visionary and unwavering B.I.G. ("Belief In God") faith. For these and other reasons, I am supporting without hesitation and with great anticipation his candidacy for President of the National Baptist Convention, USA, Inc.

Reverend Dr. Cullian W. Hill
Greater Concord Missionary Baptist Church
Detroit, Michigan

Greater Concord Missionary Baptist Church is located in Detroit, Michigan. Reverend Dr. Cullian W. Hill organized the church on April 12, 1981. Dr. Hill has served as the pastor since its inception.

What is your vision for the up-building and transformation of your community?

My vision for up-building and transforming of my community is to remove the burned houses, purchase the land and build houses that will enhance the community; not low income nor section eight homes, but homes that will improve the mentality of the Black race. The church must get involved in rebuilding our neighborhoods.

Why do you believe the Black church is relevant in the 21st century?

To be relevant, the 21st century church must think "outside of the box."

Why do you support Reverend Dr. R.B. Holmes Jr. for the presidency of the National Baptist Convention USA?

Dr. R. B. Holmes Jr. is a 21st century thinker. Dr. Holmes served ten years of dynamic leadership to our National Baptist Congress of Christian Education. He is the man with the vision for the 21st century. No other candidate has leadership qualities that Dr. Holmes has. That's why I am honored to be on his ticket as vice president at large for the National Baptist Convention USA, Inc.

Reverend Johnny T. Johnson
Philadelphia Missionary Baptist Church
Jacksonville, Florida

The Philadelphia Missionary Baptist Church is located in Jacksonville, Florida. The church has been in existence for about 100 years. Reverend Johnny T. Johnson has served as the pastor for the past five years.

What is your vision for the up-building and transformation of your community?

My vision for the up-building and transformation of our community lies in the fact that our church is founded on the Word of God, biblical principles and prayer. Our ultimate goal and desire is to win souls for the Kingdom of God. We want to be a church with a spirit of excellence, integrity and compassion for our community, serving them with the utmost level of dignity and respect. We want to be a place of worship where the love of God is demonstrated to the lost, broken, hurting, sick, confused, depressed and suppressed. We want to teach, train, equip and develop the saints in the Word of God, enabling them to engage in spiritual warfare, conquering and defeating the enemy. We want to inspire the Saints in the Word of God to seek and serve God through living holy lives. We desire to be dedicated to academic and spiritual excellence through mentoring and by supporting spiritual leaders.

Why do you believe the Black church is relevant in the 21st century?

I believe that the Black church is relevant in the 21st century because I know that without the Black church, Black people will perish. They will forget who they are and will not be taught from whence they came. Having pastored Philadelphia Missionary Baptist Church for the last five years, I've learned that there is still a need for leaders who are dedicated and committed to telling our people what the truth of the gospel is. Our people are being led astray by too many false hopes. It's time to get back to business in the 21st century and move the Black church from a profitable concept back to the true gospel; the gospel that was brought forth by the prophets and fulfilled by the Savior; and the gospel of Jesus Christ who was crucified for all of us.

Why do you support Reverend Dr. R.B. Holmes Jr. for the presidency of the National Baptist Convention USA?

I support Dr. R. B. Holmes Jr. for the office of president of the National Baptist Convention, USA because I believe that he is a man of integrity. He is one that I know can get the job done. His leadership abilities are impeccable. He has done it before; and I know, he can do it again.

Reverend Dr. Roosevelt T. Joyner
Koinonia Baptist Church Inc.
Memphis, Tennessee

Reverend Dr. Roosevelt T. Joyner is the founder and pastor of Koinonia Baptist Church, Inc. located in Memphis, Tennessee.

What is your vision for the up-building and transformation of your community?

My vision for the community is to choose capable leadership who is really concerned about making our community better. I believe in leaders who are not self-serving or narcissistic and who have an altruistic view of really making the community better. In putting things in perspective:

1. It begins with the family. The Black family must play a strategic role in up-building the community.

2. The church must do more than just praise and worship, but have and implement holistic actions for making the community better.

3. Local and national leaders must come together with concrete strategies to implement in making all communities better.

Why do you believe the Black church is relevant in the 21st century?

The role of the church has not changed and will continue to be relevant in the 21st century. However, we must rethink the way we do things. For example, church leaders must continue to play an active role in electing political leaders that are concerned about educational programs in public and private schools, humanitarian efforts, rehabilitation, prison ministries, etc.

Why do you support Reverend Dr. R.B. Holmes Jr. for the presidency of the National Baptist Convention USA?

I support Dr. R. B. Holmes Jr. for the presidency of the National Baptist Convention USA, Inc. because I believe that he has the only clear vision for making a change. I think he will work hard to make a difference. I have found Dr. Holmes to be tenacious, considerate, compassionate, and a mover and a shaker that can make things happen.

Reverend Dr. Frederick Douglas Newbill
First Timothy Baptist Church
Jacksonville, Florida

The First Timothy Baptist Church is located in Jacksonville, Florida. The church has been in existence for about 53 years. Reverend Dr. Frederick Douglas Newbill has served as pastor for the past 27 years.

What is your vision for the up-building and transformation of your community?

My vision is to find ways to magnify economic development. For instance, most of our money in the Black community of Jacksonville comes in and goes out of the community since we don't have basic grocery stores, malls and businesses. It does not have an opportunity to change hands in the community like other communities in the city. I think the National Baptist Convention USA is vital in this area because of the number of churches that are part of the convention with the opportunity to establish economic development among cities. Every city has a plan as it relates to economic development. Every city gives money to promote private enterprise. Every city, each day is voting to give dollars to corporations and businesses to hire people, but many of these opportunities do not have an effect on our community. So, we have to establish a power base to speak to our community about the benefit of voting and paying taxes. Since everybody pays taxes, the money that we invest in private enterprise also has to be distributed fairly so that the African American community can also be revitalized and built up like other communities.

Why do you believe the Black church is relevant in the 21st century?

I believe the Black church is relevant because it is the only entity that we literally own, and it still has the vision of evangelizing our community. The Black church is relevant because it has the message of transformation. Once the Black church touches a person, he or she becomes transformed. No matter what the person was before, he or she ends up working and going back to school and becoming a productive part of our community. The Black church still has a fresh word and has not lost sight of what it takes in order for us to reach out to people in the 21st century.

The Black church belongs to everybody in the community. We are living in a day that a Black preacher does more than just preach on Sunday. To meet the needs of people in the community, you see the Black preacher now dealing with our family issues, inspiring our young people and addressing the power to be in our community. The Black church continues to be visionary and in touch with what is required of it in this millennium.

Why do you support Reverend Dr. R.B. Holmes Jr. for the presidency of the National Baptist Convention USA?

I support Reverend Holmes because he has already done in his community what needs to be done in our convention. Rev. Holmes has spoken the vision. He has gone out and taken the community around him where the whole community was dilapidated and home sales were non-existed. He was able to take that property, build homes and restore the community again. He also revitalized the community by opening a restaurant, mall and school. He looked at our citizenry and said, "We will not throw away our community." Subsequently, he built a senior citizen's living facility and staffed it with people who care and make sure that the residents are comfortable in their surroundings.

Knowing that there was a mental health issue in our community, Reverend Holmes did not close his eyes and let the state take care of the matter, he hired people to build a family life building and hired professionals such as a psychologist and others to address the problem.

In lieu of talking about doing thing to improve our community, Reverend Holmes has done it. He set a pattern for creating and transforming schools in our community. For example, he has one of the oldest charter schools in Florida that is successful as evident by the state school grade. Reverend Holmes covers all sectors of our community such as education, economic development, business revitalization, community and home revitalization, home ownership, mental health services, etc. This is the type of person we need to have as president of the National Baptist Convention because he has already done things that are needed for the convention.

Reverend Holmes is ready to do it again for our communities across the nation. He has worked hard and the Lord has blessed him in revitalizing our community and in other areas of his predilection. For example, he owns a radio station, newspaper and other things. That is the kind person we want who has already succeeded. Everything he has done is above board. Everything he will continue to do will be above board. I support him because he understands the Black church, and his heart is to help our churches throughout the nation replicate ministries he has done in his community. Reverend Holmes has contacts of people of power such as the NFL and NBA. He has the ability to bring them into the picture along with charities and non-profit organizations that can give million dollars to support our communities.

All of this is being brought to the table to help churches, not just in suburban areas but also churches in rural areas. Consequently, I support Reverend Holmes who is a man of vision and integrity. He is a man who has already done what he is saying that need to be done in our communities nationwide rather a man who is saying what we need to do and has never done anything. I support him because of his proven credibility. As a friend, I have seen him as president of One Church, One Child where we put hundreds of thousands of children in Black homes. I have seen him operate as the head of our State Congress. I have seen him operate as the head of our National Congress. I have seen him operate at his local church. He is the man for the time. Such a time like this, I believe God has set Reverend Holmes aside to be our next president of the National Baptist Convention USA. And I support him wholeheartedly.

Reverend Dr. Daniel Simmons
Mt. Zion Baptist Church, Albany, Georgia

The Mt. Zion Baptist Church (MZBC) is located in Albany, Georgia. Reverend Dr. Daniel Simmons has served as senior pastor of MZBC since 1991. Simmons and the congregation of Mt. Zion demonstrate a commitment to making disciples for Jesus Christ (Matthew 28:18-20) and ministry to the "Least of These" (Matthew 25:34-40).

What is your vision for the up-building and transformation of your community?

It is my belief that the church should be about the business of transforming communities through a spiritual transformation such as preaching of the Gospel. We believe in Roman 12: 1-2 that we ought to be transformed by the renewing of our minds, so we can do what is good and acceptable of God. In addition to preaching the Gospel, I believe that transformation takes place through teaching and giving people the opportunity to get involved in ministry. As result of spiritual transformation, every other part of a person's life is impacted socially in terms of community, family, economics and education. Everything changes once the spiritual transformation takes place in a person's livelihood.

Why do you believe the Black church is relevant in the 21st century?

I don't think about it as a Black or White church. I just do church. The church period is relevant for the 21st century. It has always been relevant. It is no different from the first century to the 21st century. The church is the only institution in the world that God has entrusted as the salvation for the world. Regardless of the type of church (Black, White or Brown), it will never lose its relevancy. Nobody else in this world has a commission from God to save this world but the church.

Why do you support Reverend Dr. R.B. Holmes Jr. for the presidency of the National Baptist Convention USA?

I have known Reverend Holmes for 20 years. I worked with him during his tenure as president of the National Baptist Congress of Christian Education (NBCCE). While in Albany, Georgia, I am close enough to Tallahassee to be aware of what he is doing at Bethel Missionary Baptist Church (BMBC). Based on Reverend Holmes' work at BMBC for 27 years and NBCCE for 10 years, I believe that he has all of the tools necessary to make a good president for the National Baptist Convention USA. I think his experience matters as a pastor and proven leader at the Congress level. I think the relationships he built over the years of people in and outside of our convention makes a difference as well.

4. The Holmes Education Post's Interview of Reverend Dr. R.B. Holmes Jr.

What career path led to your profession or interest in becoming president of the National Baptist Convention, USA, Inc.?

I have been pastor of Bethel Missionary Baptist Church in Tallahassee, Florida for 27 years, pastor of First Timothy Baptist Church in Jacksonville, Florida for 10 years, past president of the National Baptist Congress of Christian Education for 10 years and past president of Congress of Christian Education for the Florida General Baptist Convention for six years. These experiences, coupled with a wealth of community service activities have led to my journey to become president of the National Baptist Convention, USA. As we know, "all things work together for good to them that love God, to them who are called according to his purpose" (Romans 8:28). I believe God is calling me for this purpose: "that he which hath begun a good work in you will perform it until the day of Jesus Christ" (Philippians 1:6).

What educational background and/or professional training are essential for becoming president of the National Baptist Convention, USA, Inc.?

I believe you must have a good educational background. I have received an Associate of Arts degree from Central Florida Junior College, a Bachelor of Arts degree from Malone College, a Master of Arts degree from Methodist Theological Seminary and a doctoral degree from Virginia Union University.

What influenced you to pursue a career as president of the National Baptist Convention, USA, Inc.?

After much prayer and reflection, I have decided to seek the presidency of the National Baptist Convention, USA, Inc. in 2014. I strongly and humbly believe that I have the vision, strengths, gifts and experience to build and re-energize our great National Convention. My prayerful decision in seeking this office is simply because I believe I have the right spirit, attitude and leadership skills to lead the National Convention for this season.

We are living in some critical and challenging times: It is important that the National Baptist Convention becomes a stronger voice and have a compelling vision that will save, strengthen and sustain Black Baptist churches. I believe that I can lead this

National Convention to provide ministries and services that will meet the needs of our churches in the 21st Century.

It is true that, "Where there is no vision, the people perish" (Proverbs 29:18). Our beloved members and churches are hurting; therefore, we need a stronger and more vibrant National Convention presence and programs. I firmly believe that the Lord, Jesus Christ, has uniquely prepared me to serve "For such a time as this" (Esther 4:14).

What advice do you give to students who desire to become a president of the National Baptist Convention, USA, Inc.?

For students who desire to become a president of the National Convention, I encourage them to let it be a calling from God. And when that time comes, be prepared spiritually, educationally, socially and physically to fulfill the needs of the convention with a strong vision and conviction.

What professional, civic, or community organizations do you belong?

Among some of my activities, I am member of the Board of Trustees for Edward Waters College, Florida Memorial University and Malone University, as well as past member of the Board of Trustees for Florida A&M University. Providing additional support to the community and educational institutions, I am chairman and founder of the National Save the Family Now Movement, Inc. and the National Anti-Hazing/Anti-Violence Task Force. Furthermore, I am president of the Southeast Region for the National Newspaper Publishers Association, president of the Tallahassee Chapter of the National Action Network and recipients of the Gubernatorial Appointments by Governors Bob Graham, Bob Martinez, Lawton Chiles, Jeb Bush, Charlie Crist and Rick Scott.

Describe your vision for the National Baptist Convention, USA, Inc.?

For the rebuilding and reinvigoration of the National Baptist Convention, USA, Inc., the Lord has blessed me with the "12-Point Action Plan Vision" as highlighted in Chapter I. In fact, I believe this vision is achievable because "with God, nothing is impossible" (Luke 1:37).

Why should churches have Christian Charter Schools?

We have been called and commissioned by God to "Train up a child in the way he should go, and when he is old, he will not depart from it:" Proverbs 22:6. This is an awesome responsibility for both parents and preachers. God has given us a mandate and a mission to train children in the right way. It is asinine to think that we can get this job done once a week, in Sunday School, for about 30 minutes. The training of a child to walk right, to talk right and to do the right thing is a lifetime job.

In the book of Deuteronomy (6:7-10), Moses laid out the instruction that the Jewish people were to provide for their children: "And thou shalt teach them diligently unto thy children; and shalt talk of them while thou sittest in thine house, and when thou walkest by the way, and when thou liest down, and when thou risest up. And thou shalt bind them for a sign upon thine hand, and they shall be as frontlets between thine eyes. And thou shalt write them upon the posts of thy house, and on thy gates."

So through Christian Charter Schools, we have to teach the word of God; teach the importance of excelling academically; and to teach our own history, from a spiritual and Afrocentric point of view.

How will you partner with other denominations to glory the Kingdom of God?

If we are going to bring communities together, there has to be a new commitment to break down denominations and racial barriers. As a Christian community, we serve one Lord, one Faith and one Baptism. I think that it is not a sin to support denominational diversity and inclusion. I believe that my experience working with various groups, politically, socially, economically and evangelically, has strategically and uniquely prepared me to be a voice for religious togetherness and harmony.

REFERENCES

Holmes, R.B. Jr. (2000). *The private Christian school in the African-American Church: It is needed. Tallahassee, FL: Sentry Press.*

King James Version. Holy Bible.

National Baptist Convention USA, Inc. Election and voting. Retrieved February 24, 2014 from, http://www.nationalbaptist.com/about-us/elections--voting.html

U. S. Department of Labor (2012). Unemployment in June 2012. Retrieved April 14, 2014 from, http://www/bls.gov/opub/ted/2012/ted_20120710.htm

U.S. Census Bureau (2010). Income, Poverty and Health Insurance Coverage in the United States: 2010. Retrieved April 14, 2014 from, http://www.census.gov/newsroom/releases/archives/ income_wealth/cb11-157.html

AUTHOR'S BACKGROUND

Ronald Holmes is the author of five books: "Education Questions to be Answered," "Current Issues and Answers in Education," "How to Eradicate Hazing," "Professional Career Paths" and "Your Answers to Education Questions." He is the sponsoring editor for the landmark book, "Surviving and Thriving: Candid, Real Life Stories of Prostate Cancer."

Ronald Holmes is president and publisher of The Holmes Education Post, an education focused Internet newspaper. His philanthropist spirit and unselfish giving has enabled him to provide free educational resources and publications to educators across the nation. He publishes weekly articles on educational issues and offers unique, researched based solutions, perspectives, best practices and resources to improve public education.

Ronald Holmes is a member of the National Association of School Superintendents, national superintendent of the National Save the Family Now Movement, Inc. and vice president and education editor of Live Communications, Inc. (Capital Outlook Newspaper and WTAL 1450 AM). He earned a Ph.D. in Educational Leadership, a ME.D. in Educational Administration and Supervision and a B.S. in Business Education from Florida A&M University. He also earned a ME.D. in Business Education from Bowling Green State University. He has proven success working from the elementary to the collegiate level.

Ronald Holmes is a native of Jacksonville, Florida and married to Constance Holmes. He is an avid jogger and enjoys competitive races.